Fasting
&
Stewardship

Look for these topics in the
Everyday Matters Bible Studies for Women

Acceptance

Bible Study & Meditation

Celebration

Community

Confession

Contemplation

Faith

Fasting

Forgiveness

Gratitude

Hospitality

Justice

Mentoring

Outreach

Prayer

Reconciliation

Sabbath & Rest

Service

Silence

Simplicity

Solitude

Stewardship

Submission

Worship

Fasting & Stewardship

Spiritual Practices
FOR EVERYDAY LIFE

HENDRICKSON
PUBLISHERS

Everyday Matters Bible Studies for Women—
Fasting & Stewardship

© 2014 Hendrickson Publishers Marketing, LLC
P. O. Box 3473
Peabody, Massachusetts 01961-3473

ISBN 978-1-61970-442-8

Printed in the United States of America

Second Printing — August 2014

Contents

Stewardship

Holy Habits

Spiritual Practices for Everyday Life

Everyday life today is busier and more distracting than it has ever been before. While cell phones and texting make it easier to keep track of children and each other, they also make it harder to get away from the demands that overwhelm us. Time, it seems, is a shrinking commodity. But God, the Creator of time, has given us the keys to leading a life that may be challenging but not overwhelming. In fact, he offers us tools to do what seems impossible and come away refreshed and renewed. These tools are called spiritual practices, or spiritual disciplines.

Spiritual practices are holy habits. They are rooted in God's word, and they go back to creation itself. God has hardwired us to thrive when we obey him, even when it seems like his instructions defy our "common sense." When we engage in the holy habits that God has ordained, time takes on a new dimension. What seems impossible is actually easy; it's easy because we are tapping into God's resources.

The holy habits that we call spiritual practices are all geared to position us in a place where we can allow the Holy Spirit to work in us and through us, to grant us power and strength to do the things we can't do on our own. They take us to a place where we can become intimate with God.

While holy habits and everyday life may sound like opposites, they really aren't.

As you learn to incorporate spiritual practices into your life, you'll find that everyday life is easier. At the same time, you will draw closer to God and come to a place where you can luxuriate in his rich blessings. Here is a simple example. Elizabeth Collings hated running household errands. Picking up dry cleaning, doing the grocery shopping, and chauffeuring her kids felt like a never-ending litany of menial chores. One day she had a simple realization that changed her life. That day she began to use her "chore time" as a time of prayer and fellowship with God.

Whenever Elizabeth walked the aisle of the supermarket, she prayed for each person who would eat the item of food she selected. On her way to pick up her children, she would lay their lives out before God, asking him to be there for them even when she couldn't. Each errand became an opportunity for fellowship with God. The chore that had been so tedious became a precious part of her routine that she cherished.

The purpose of these study guides is to help you use spiritual practices to make your own life richer, fuller, and deeper. The series includes twenty-four spiritual practices that are the building blocks of Christian spiritual formation. Each practice is a holy habit that has been modeled for us in the Bible. The practices are acceptance, Bible study and meditation, celebration, community, confession, contemplation, faith, fasting, forgiveness, gratitude, hospitality, justice, mentoring, outreach, prayer, reconciliation, Sabbath and rest, service, silence, simplicity, solitude, stewardship, submission, and worship.

As you move through the practices that you select, remember Christ's promise in Matthew 11:28–30:

> *Come to me, all of you who are weary and carry heavy burdens. Take my yoke upon you. Let me teach you, because I am humble and gentle at heart, and you will find rest for your souls. For my yoke is easy to bear, and the burden I give you is light.*

Introduction

to the Practice of Fasting & Stewardship

> The gentlest form of spiritual narcissism is the idea that one can accomplish one's own spiritual growth. . . . The belief that "I can do it" is intimately associated with the assumption that "it is my idea, my desire, to do it." Spiritual narcissism works to deny the realization that our spirituality comes from God. —Gerald May

Though we live in a land of plenty, we often look at our lives through the lens of what we lack. Global statistics bear out our affluence: even those of us making the minimum wage in America make more than 93 percent of the world (www.globalrichlist com). Our average home size is larger, we have more leisure time, our general health is better, our lives are longer, and our educational level is higher. So why do we generally see our resources as scarce and allow worry and fear to rule so many of our daily decisions?

This mind-set is fostered by the barrage of media messages and our consumer-driven economy. But our history is also a culprit—we are a culture of people who have always tended to be dissatisfied with the status quo. More freedom, more liberty, more land—it's a national persona that honors striving and discontent. And we must be honest: the discontent has proven to be a successful way to build up and build out a country.

Yet the very real danger for us, as we follow the way of Jesus, is to take on a mind-set of both scarcity and self-control. Scarcity breeds thoughts such as *there's only so much to go around.* We'd better take what we can, save all we can, keep all we can. Self-control takes our dissatisfaction and tells us: *If anything is going to change to the good in our lives, it's up to us to make it happen.*

Let's turn away from these thoughts and turn back to the Scriptures—full of the wise counsel of a Father who knows us, truly knows us and what we need to thrive. Rather than scarcity and control, God's gift to us is abundance and his eternal presence. Against the cacophony of commands the world offers us every day God speaks to us from the Scriptures:

> *"Be careful to obey all the commands I am giving you today. Then you will live and multiply, and you will enter and occupy the land the Lord swore to give your ancestors. Remember how the Lord your God led you through the wilderness for these forty years, humbling you and testing you to prove your character, and to find out whether or not you would obey his commands. Yes, he humbled you by letting you go hungry and then feeding you with manna, a food previously unknown to you and your ancestors. He did it to teach you that people do not live by bread alone; rather, we live by*

every word that comes from the mouth of the Lord. For all
these forty years your clothes didn't wear out, and your feet
didn't blister or swell. Think about it: Just as a parent disci-
plines a child, the Lord your God disciplines you for your own
good." (Deuteronomy 8:1–5)

As he did with the Israelites, so he does with us. He leads us
to practices for living well, practices that lead us to patterns
of dependence and gratitude. Included among those biblical
practices are stewardship and fasting—concepts in danger
of becoming far too seasonal and restricted in our faith life.

For many of us, "stewardship" is a word trotted out but once
a year by the finance committee at church, as they set the
vision and plans for the coming year. And through such
constant limited use, it's also become synonymous with our
money and how much we give. But stewardship is a practice
far richer for the believer, far more valuable for spiritual
formation than we allow. It's time to redeem the word and
the practice, and understand God's plan to use it to create a
whole-hearted follower.

Much the same can be said about fasting. For most of us,
it's one of those ideas that sounds good as long as someone else is doing it. And we come by that naturally; it is so
counterintuitive to deny our bodies its basic needs, it's easy
to conclude such a discipline should be reserved for the
most drastic, catastrophic situations. And yet our brothers
and sisters in Christ through the centuries have practiced
this discipline regularly. As with the discipline of stewardship, it's time to return to the Scriptures and reimagine the
discipline of fasting for our day-to-day faith life.

Fasting

CHAPTER 1

Why Should We Fast?

Seeking Less in a Life of Too Much

> LORD, we show our trust in you by obeying your laws;
> our heart's desire is to glorify your name.
> All night long I search for you;
> in the morning I earnestly seek for God.
> For only when you come to judge the earth
> will people learn what is right.
>
> ISAIAH 26:8-9

For this study, read Isaiah 26.

In my early adulthood, both my weight and my finances were strained. I weighed far too much and owed far too much, which led to a lot of anxiety and discomfort. And yet when I tried to rein in either area—go on a diet or set a budget—the result was I felt pinched, like I was trying to squeeze my life into a small container, which then made me resentful. When the focus turned to what I could not eat and what I could not buy, it didn't take long for that rebellious part of me to say, "Who says that's all you can have?

Why are you doing this to yourself? Your life is meant to be made of bigger things!"

When I finally stopped doing to myself what I would never have done to another, I knew I needed help and a regular plan. In both my finances and weight, there were helpful organizations I turned to; and no surprise, the first thing they did was set budgets, both caloric and financial. Again, I felt pinched. But this time, instead of allowing the rebellion, I submitted—again and again, daily—to the limitations of the budget. The result, after years of submission to a plan not my own, was freedom. I stopped saying to myself, "That's all you can have." The phrase had become instead, "Wow, that's all you really need."

This is why we fast. We fast to come, finally, to the place where we realize we have all that we really need. Alise Barrymore states in the *Everyday Matters Bible for Women* that fasting "reminds us how vulnerable and dependent we are on God." And yet in that dependence, we realize the sufficiency of God in our lives.

We realize the daily bread in the Lord's Prayer is the same Jesus, the Bread of Life of John 6:35. We can trust Jesus when he says, "Whoever comes to me will never be hungry again."

Our exercise of the discipline of fasting filters into our whole lives, into other disciplines such as stewardship, submission, Sabbath-keeping, and worship. As Dallas Willard writes in the *Spirit of the Disciplines*, "Since food has the pervasive place it does in our lives, the effects of fasting will be diffused throughout our personality. It the midst of all our needs and wants, we experience the contentment of the child that has been weaned from its mother's breast." When we master, with God's help, control of our appetite, making it yield to its Maker, we master so many other areas that fight for control as well.

We find encouragement for the need for fasting in both Old and New Testaments. In Leviticus 23:32, when the Lord talks about the Sabbath, he says, "And on that day you must deny yourselves." Included perhaps is the idea of denying of food or perhaps a limited diet. And I love the example we have in Acts of the early church. In Acts 13:1–3, Luke reports the following:

> *Among the prophets and teachers of the church at Antioch of Syria were Barnabas, Simeon (called "the black man"), Lucius (from Cyrene), Manaen (the childhood companion of King Herod Antipas), and Saul. One day as these men were worshiping the Lord and fasting, the Holy Spirit said, "Dedicate Barnabas and Saul for the special work to which I have called them." So after more fasting and prayer, the men laid their hands on them and sent them on their way.*

Fasting and worship, happening together—fasting that brings us to our dependence on God, and then leads us to praise the all-sufficiency of God. What a beautiful picture for us as we yield our lives daily to God.

We fast also "for the sake of intense spiritual activity" as Richard Foster says in the *Everyday Matters Bible for Women*. There are times when the need is critical, and our most urgent need for God's intervention can only be expressed by fasting. The Bible gives us several examples. In

Jonah 3, the king of Nineveh commands the entire town to fast with the hope that "perhaps even yet God will change his mind and hold back his fierce anger from destroying us" (Jonah 3:9). In 2 Chronicles 20, Jehoshaphat directs the people of Judah to fast and seek deliverance from the armies marching toward them. And in Deuteronomy 9:18–19, Moses reminds the people: "I ate no bread and drank no water because of the great sin you had committed by doing what the LORD hated, provoking him to anger. I feared that the furious anger of the LORD, which turned him against you, would drive him to destroy you." When times of crisis come to us, already having a habit of fasting means we can reflexively move into a posture of dependence on God. In the Bible, when the need is great, men and women don't seem to spend much time wringing their hands, asking "Why me? Why now?" or finding another solution. They seem to immediately move to fast and pray.

The same response is available to us. In plenty and in want, in worship and in need, fasting is part of the way we express our dependence on God.

"Fasting is a critical discipline for the life of the spirit— through fasting we respond in obedience to God's urgings, we come to know ourselves (and our sins) more fully, and we turn to God in complete reliance as we seek his will in difficult situations." —Richard J. Foster, "Why Fast?" Everyday Matters Bible for Women

As you study this chapter, consider your own faith life. How much of it seems to be about restricting your actions? How much is about realizing what you need?

1. In his reflection in the *Everyday Matters Bible for Women*, Ben Patterson says that fasting gave him permission "to not have to live on the level of my appetites," and when the fast ended, his biggest fear was "I might lose the freedom I'd gained." What about you? What could you find freedom from by fasting?

2. Consider the passages of John 6:35, Deuteronomy 8:3, and Matthew 4:1–2. How does the image of being fed by the word of God help you undertake a fast?

3. Think of a time of intense spiritual activity in your life. What was your response?

4. What are the reasons you might fast?

5. How do you see the spiritual disciplines of fasting and worship working together to strengthen your faith? Do you think one discipline helps with the other?

6. In Leviticus 23:32 God required the Israelites, as part of their Sabbath, to "deny themselves." What would you deny yourself of to achieve a complete rest?

———————————— ❧ ————————————

"The greatest enemy of hunger for God is not poison but apple pie. It is not the banquet of the wicked that dulls our appetite for heaven, but endless nibbling at the table of the world. It is not the X-rated video, but the prime-time dribble of triviality we drink in every night." —John Piper

Points to Ponder

The practice of fasting is new to many of us. Because it's a spiritual discipline, we want to get it right. We want a list to follow. Though there are different kinds of fasts discussed in Scripture, we would be better off stopping ourselves from this line of thinking altogether.

* First, reflect on the *why*: Why do people fast?

* What benefit can it have for you?

Prayer

O Lord, you are the source of all I have, all I want, and all I need. Today let me see the world with your eyes. Let me know my true dependence on you and your trustworthiness.

Add your prayer in your own words.

Amen.

Put It into Practice

This week, ask a few people you trust and admire about their experiences with fasting. Why do they fast? What did their fast consist of? Jot down your own reflections after discussing.

Take-away Treasure

God daily provides all we need. This week, consider all the ways you can change your thoughts and words from statements of scarcity (all I can have) to contentment (all I need).

> *If there is no element of asceticism in our lives, if we give free rein to the desires of the flesh (taking care of course to keep within the limits of what seems permissible to the world), we shall find it hard to train for the service of Christ. When the flesh is satisfied it is hard to pray with cheerfulness or to devote oneself to a life of service which calls for much self-renunciation.*
> —*Dietrich Bonhoeffer*, The Cost of Discipleship

CHAPTER 2

When Should We Fast?

Seeking God in Ordinary and Extraordinary Times

> Even though the fig trees have no blossoms,
>   and there are no grapes on the vines;
> even though the olive crop fails,
>   and the fields lie empty and barren;
> even though the flocks die in the fields,
>   and the cattle barns are empty,
> yet I will rejoice in the Lord!
>   I will be joyful in the God of my salvation!
> The Sovereign Lord is my strength!
>   He makes me as surefooted as a deer,
>   able to tread upon the heights.

HABAKKUK 3:17

For this study, read Habakkuk 3.

My few attempts at fasting thus far have been inspired but undisciplined. I would read a book or hear a message that moved me, emotionally at least, to want the experience of a fast—a spiritual high point, an epiphany, and a sense of being closer to God. So I would decide the next day to go without food, and by mid-morning my only focal point was food and coffee. By lunch the fast was abandoned.

In hindsight, I can see the many ways my approach was doomed to failure. I wasn't seeking God. I was seeking an experience, using fasting as a magic key to open a door to a different relationship with God, some sort of "insider's" world. It was the very kind of thing Paul warned the Colossians about, reminding them it is Christ alone who saves, not additional experiences of Christ, that "in him lie hidden all the treasures of wisdom and knowledge" (Colossians 2:3). I also wasn't prepared because I wasn't in the habit of denying myself. I had a twenty-first-century American body used to getting its full caloric needs met each and every day.

Throughout Scripture as we read about people fasting, it's good to remember two things. First, on any given day, the Israelites were eating less and leaner food than we tend to. In his book *Jesus and the Gospels,* New Testament scholar Craig Blomberg writes that 70 percent of the population lived at a level we would consider poverty. They knew hunger as a companion in ways we do not, so their bodies started, of necessity, from a more disciplined place. Second, they fasted regularly. When the Bible mentions fasting, early readers would know, and would have experienced, that these were not the *only* times of fasting. There were the recorded times, but as Frederica Mathewes-Green notes in her article "Fasting Like the Early Church?" in the *Everyday Matters Bible for Women,* both the Jews and early Christians fasted twice a week.

> In church history early Christians made it a habit to fast
> together. . . . The Didache reminds believers that the Jews
> fast on Tuesdays and Thursdays. . . . But the Didache does

not say, "So avoid that fasting foolishness, because we don't need it." No, this earliest church-discipline text instructs that Christians should fast as well, but on Wednesdays (the day of Judas's betrayal) and Fridays (the day of the Crucifixion).

Fasting, basically, was happening all the time in the Bible. And why not? In the most immediate way, it reminds us how dependent we are on God's provision. And in a way, it does unlock a mystery about God, but not the one I was seeking. Like all the disciplines, it points us fully to the pre-eminence of God in our lives. And by doing so, fasting offers us freedom from being our own gods.

Scripture as well records several events that compelled God's people to fast. As Alise Barrymore notes in the *Everyday Matters Bible for Women*:

In the Scriptures people often fasted purposefully—with a specific reason in mind. For example, people would fast when someone was experiencing private affliction, such as David who fasted when his child was ill (2 Samuel 12:15–17), and when danger was approaching, such as when Esther, along with all the Jews in Persia, fasted as she prepared for her dangerous meeting with King Xerxes (Esther 4:15–16). Other reasons people fasted were the ordination of ministers (Acts 13:2–3); confession of sin (1 Samuel 7:6; Nehemiah 9:1–2); seeking humility (Psalm 35:13); to discern God's will and direction (Ezra 8:21–23); to seek healing (Isaiah 58:6–8); to request God's intervention (2 Chronicles 20:3); in obedience to the direction of a leader (Jonah 3:6–10).

According to the Bible, we fast both in ordinary and extraordinary times.

> *"The purpose of fasting is to loosen to some degree the ties which bind us to the world of material things and our surroundings as a whole, in order that we may concentrate all our spiritual powers upon the unseen and eternal things." —Ole Hallesby*

As you study this chapter, don't be surprised to find a part of you agreeing in theory to the idea of fasting but resistant to the actual practice. Stop and allow yourself to consider why it's so difficult to fast.

1. Perhaps you, too, see the wisdom of fasting as a regular discipline. Look at your weekly schedule—are there one or two days best suited for you to try a modified fast?

2. How often does your church encourage fasting? Are there others within your body of believers who can gather to encourage one another in this practice?

3. Richard Foster writes, "We fast because there's an urgent need. Sometimes drastic situations demand a drastic response, such as intense fasting as part of our prayer for a crisis or difficulty. A spiritually disciplined person will know when a situation requires the intense supplication of fasting." Has there been a time (or times) in your life where you felt driven to fast? What was your urgent need? Do you feel fasting helped?

4. There can be many purposes for a fast other than an urgent situation. What are other reasons for fasting? What could be *your* reason?

5. Read Psalm 35 in its entirety. Within the full context of the psalm, when did David fast and why? In what other ways did he express himself in this psalm?

6. In her article "Rest and Self-Denial?" in the *Everyday Matters Bible for Women*, Kelli Trujillo suggests other things we can fast from, such as sexual expression, makeup, or "screen time" as we call it—anything with a screen, from TV to computers to tablets. Are there fasts other than food you might consider?

"Those which were figures [in the Old Testament] of future things have passed away, what they signified being accomplished. But the utility of fasting is not done away with in the New Testament; but it is piously observed, that fasting is always profitable both to the soul and body." —St. Leo

---

Points to Ponder

Part of fasting is training your body to be subject to the will, preparing it to be used as part of your worship and service to God. While we don't only fast, it is one of the tools we can use to place ourselves in a posture of dependence.

- Write down some times in which you've needed training—sports, work skills, perhaps other spiritual disciplines.

- How can the lessons you've learned in those areas be helpful to you as you prepare yourself for fasting?

"Food is ultimately not about food, but about God. The meaning of hunger—indeed, of all desire—is to point us to God." —Ben Patterson

---

Prayer

Your steadfast love and provision for me, Lord, never end. I want to stay in a posture of dependence and gratitude every day, not just once in a while. May my habits and practices today keep me ever mindful of your care.

Add your prayer in your own words.

Amen.

Put It into Practice

Consider the month before you and how you might take the next thirty days to prepare yourself for fasting. Think of it as a training month. How can you increase your physical tolerance for fasting during this time?

Take-away Treasure

Look at the prayer needs you've written down or that have been shared at your church. Ask God for his guidance. Is there a need calling you to fast? The answer might be no, and it might be an obvious yes. The goal is to begin to be open to God's promptings in the matter of fasting on a regular basis.

True fasting, as the divine Master repeats elsewhere, is rather to do the will of the Heavenly Father, who "sees in secret, and will reward you" (Mt 6, 18). He Himself sets the example, answering Satan, at the end of the forty days spent in the desert that "man shall not live by bread alone, but by every word that proceeds from the mouth of God" (Mt 4, 4). The true fast is thus directed to eating the "true food," which is to do the Father's will (cf. Jn 4, 34). —Pope Benedict XVI

CHAPTER 3

How Should We Fast?

Seeking More of God

"People judge by outward appearance,
but the LORD looks at the heart."

1 SAMUEL 16:7

For this study, read Matthew 6:1–18.

Right now at our house we're navigating the world of college applications, as are many of our friends. Recently I asked another mom about how her son reported his volunteer work on the application. She gave an exasperated sigh and shook her head. "He isn't reporting any of his volunteer hours," she said. "His feeling is if he gets any reward for volunteering, even if it's just listing it as an activity on his college application, then it's not a true volunteer effort. It's something he's doing in order to get something in return."

Wow. Her son is right, and both his answer and my own astonishment told me just how hard it is to keep our motives pure. Whether it's wearing our "I gave blood today" sticker or having our name listed as a donor to an event, making sure we're recognized as a Sunday school teacher or posting our latest projects on our Pinterest board, the encouragement to broadcast ourselves and our accomplishments is rife in our culture. With our smartphones and tablets at the ready, it's all too easy and tempting to push "Send" and "Post" about our every good thought and deed.

As we move into the discipline of fasting, we will look into some of the ways Scripture describes the act of fasting. But the most important issue is the one Jesus raises in the Sermon on the Mount. It's our motives for fasting that matter above all else. In Matthew 6:16–18, Jesus tells his disciples:

> *"And when you fast, don't make it obvious, as the hypocrites do, for they try to look miserable and disheveled so people will admire them for their fasting. I tell you the truth, that is the only reward they will ever get. But when you fast, comb your hair and wash your face. Then no one will notice that you are fasting, except your Father, who knows what you do in private. And your Father, who sees everything, will reward you."*

Why are you fasting? What, really, are you hoping for as you fast? Do we expect, as Kelli Trujillo discusses in the *Everyday Matters Bible for Women*, a "counterintuitive rest that fasting brings"? I'd like to aim for that.

But since that might not be where we start, I suggest we begin with the motive of obedience. We fast because it is a discipline that honors God and his preeminence in our lives. Through this act of obedience we will most likely find early on what Richard Foster notes in the *Everyday Matters Bible for Women*, that through fasting we will "come to know ourselves (and our sins) more fully." We will find just how much of who we are is tied to how we feel—are we kind and patient and generous only when we are well fed?

Here at this place of emptiness, our real work in the discipline begins. We read Jesus' words in Matthew 6 again, look at our silent Twitter feed and Facebook status, and submit to God our very real desire to let others know what we're up to. We can easily convince ourselves God would not want us to "wear a mask" and be less than authentic to a watching world. But Jesus' words in the Sermon on the Mount do not advocate a mask. He is not suggesting that by going into the world well groomed you are covering up the essential nature of who you are. Rather, you are relaxing into the abundance of God. Yes, you have not eaten; but you have submitted your body and will to God and trusted in him completely. God sees your trust and your faith. Why would we look miserable when we're safe in the arms of God?

Again and again in Scripture, believers acted in ways that pointed people to the goodness of God—healings, providing for each other, and always sharing God's plan to reconcile with us (Acts 3, 4, and 9). If they tried to take the praise for themselves, the result was never good, as happened with Ananias and Sapphira in Acts 5. We don't want to be among those Paul discusses in Romans: "Yes, they knew God, but they wouldn't worship him as God or even give him thanks. And they began to think up foolish ideas of what God was like. As a result, their minds became dark and confused" (Romans 1:21).

It is easy to want more. We know what emptiness feels like and it's not very comfortable. We easily buy into the idea of scarcity, and our souls rebel against getting less than our "fair share" of anything, whether it's food or attention. Our prayer must be to turn the feeling of a general "more" to a specific "more of God." That is a hunger God is only too happy to fill. When we fast as a way to have more of God and his rule in our lives, we come to understand, paradoxically, that we can only find it by consuming less.

"Outwardly you will be performing the regular duties of your day, but inwardly you will be in prayer and adoration, song, and worship. In a new way, cause every task of the day to be a sacred ministry to the Lord. However mundane your duties, for you they are a sacrament." —Richard Foster

---

As you study this chapter, be open to new ways to look at the practice of fasting.

1. In her reflection in the *Everyday Matters Bible,* Helen Lee says that fasting helps us to ask ourselves what we are truly hungering for. How would you answer?

2. Daniel 10:3 gives a brief outline of a modified fast. If you fasted in a way that meant you ate "no rich food" or meat or wine, what would that look like?

3. Read Isaiah 58. How does God define fasting? What passages stand out to you? Does this passage change how you see fasting in your own life?

4. In order to truly reflect the sufficiency of God, we should not look like we're suffering. For you, what does that mean? How would you go out into the world? What would you say? What would you not say?

5. John records that when the disciples urged Jesus to eat something on a very busy day, he replied that he had "a kind of food" they knew "nothing about." He then explained: "My nourishment comes from doing the will of God, who sent me, and from finishing his work." Read John 4:1–42 and write down why you think he said this.

6. Have there ever been times in your life when you felt you had "a kind of food" that no one except your Heavenly Father knew about?

Points to Ponder

Keep Matthew 6:16–18 where you can see it as you fast.

- How can you live it out as a prayer to God to keep your motives pure and to depend on him alone?

- If you've done this in the past, reflect on your experience.

"When we fast, when we deprive ourselves from the food we desire, we not only learn to lean more on God, but we are reminded physically of what our brokenness feels like. Our stomach pains reflect how our hearts ought to feel when we consider our sin. This is the role that fasting can help play in our repentance. In fasting we recognize the need we have for God in our lives—to fill us, to nourish us, and to heal our brokenness."
—Caryn Rivadeneira, "What Our Brokenness Feels Like," Everyday Matters Bible for Women

Prayer

Lord, in you alone do I find strength, and for your favor alone I fast. When I fight my own weakness, let me instead turn to you and depend on you alone.

Add your prayer in your own words.

Amen.

Put It into Practice

Look at fasting as a regular practice, leading you to dependence on God. Maybe it's a partial fast, such as Daniel had (vegetables and water!). Maybe it's a fast of food altogether but not water. Decide on a fast and try it this week. Just try it. Keep a journal to jot down your thoughts and prayers as you do.

Take-away Treasure

As you have challenged yourself to think of fasting, perhaps another area besides food keeps coming to mind. Perhaps the "fast" you need to bring you back to dependence on God has less to do with food and more to do with something else. Think about what that may be and see if you can fast from it this week.

At the end of the ten days, Daniel and his three friends looked healthier and better nourished than the young men who had been eating the food assigned by the king. (Daniel 1:15)

CHAPTER 4

When the Need Is Great

"Everyone Who Seeks, Finds"

As the deer longs for streams of water,
so I long for you, O God.
I thirst for God, the living God.
When can I go and stand before him?

PSALM 42:1-2

For this study, read Esther 4.

A few years ago our church faced a situation I can only describe as dire. A decision needed to be made, it needed to be made quickly, and getting to the decision involved moving through several prickly intersections of disappointment, unmet expectations, and immediate spiritual and physical needs. Ugh. Through many urgent phone messages, one word began and ended every phone conversation: *pray.*

Truly, I had never faced something quite like this, nor had others. This crisis was a mountain that needed to be moved. And those of us who were tasked with shepherding the issue to resolution knew our collective, desperate need for God's intervention and direction. It's fair to say we prayed without ceasing for fourteen days. The day of decision came, the congregation assembled, and still we prayed. My biggest fear is that we would damage the gospel by our actions or inactions.

God moved our mountain. What happened at our little church that day was an amazing miracle of God's provision in the lives of all of us. It was an Emmaus Road kind of moment, one that afterward had us saying, "Didn't our hearts burn within us?" (Luke 24:32). Wide-eyed, we were amazed at the mercies of God to our little band of followers; and for months after as we gathered together to worship, God's provision in our time of need was never far from our lips. Looking back I would say God didn't provide direction for the decision; instead he prepared our hearts to respond to the situation in love. And from that place, he moved us as a body in the only direction we could take if motivated by love.

You have those times too. The crisis is easy to state, the need is great and well beyond the capacity of our human powers to resolve. At such times, fasting is one of the disciplines we can turn to.

And it's not just for those who have been living faithfully with God, day in and day out, such as Queen Esther. We may be more like the wayward king of Nineveh, completely following our own dark path before turning to God in humility and dependence. Wherever we start, fasting is part of God's redemptive plan for us.

The Scriptures never tell us to shy away from telling God what we need. "For everyone who asks, receives. Everyone who seeks, finds. And to everyone who knocks, the door will be opened," says Jesus in Matthew 7:8. When James writes to believers, he encourages them to ask in ways that please God: "Yet you don't have what you want because you don't ask God for it. And even when you ask, you don't get it because your motives are all wrong—you want only what will give you pleasure" (James 4:2–3).

When we fast, God is not ignorant of the outcome we desire. As Jesus reminds us in Matthew 6:18, "Your father . . . sees everything." Fasting in response to a crisis can be about finding favor with God for the deep desires of our hearts. Esther asks for the Jews to fast along with her before she goes before the king. She doesn't fast for a decision—she fasts for favor in light of the decision to try and save the Jews in Persia (Esther 4:15–5:2). Ezra orders the exiles now returning with him Israel to fast as they prayed for a safe journey and God's care. The decision to go had been made. God's favor was their desire (Ezra 8:21–23). David as well, as he fasts and prays to God for the life of his son, is seeking God's favor: "I fasted and wept while the child was alive, for I said, 'Perhaps the LORD will be gracious to me and let the child live'" (2 Samuel 12:22).

We can come before God, in fasting and prayer, confident in him—confident in his ability to truly satisfy our deep needs, to fill with his presence all the gaps left when we are at the end of our own powers. And in doing so, we will find strength. As Nicole Unice reflects in the *Everyday Matters Bible for Women*, "When Esther fasted, she was strengthened. That same power is available to us. . . . When confronted with choices that exceed our capacity, through fasting, we draw near to a God who will sustain us with his strength."

*"Want is absolutely real. Life can absolutely turn around
in a moment. But no matter what, we can give thanks
at all times in all things because He is unchanging
and He is in control. If you are in Christ, then you are
his. And nothing else matters." —Raechel Myers*

**As you study this chapter, think about the needs
you see around you and your part in answering
those needs. Ask yourself the question Mordecai
asked Esther: Is it possible you are placed
where you are, for such a time as this?**

1. Read Deuteronomy 8:1–5 slowly. What words stand out
to you? What emotions do you connect to those words?

2. When David fasts in 2 Samuel 12, his deepest desire—for
the life of his son—is not granted. What perspective can
you gain from David's response to help you through your
own disappointments?

3. Read the book of Jonah in its entirety. When the city of Nineveh fasts upon order of the king (even the animals!), God changes his mind and the city is saved. What does such a decision tell you about the character of God?

4. Is there a critical need in your life right now?

5. When you read of Esther's fast and the actions she takes next, what do you think the benefit of the fast was for her and the Jews in Persia?

6. Have you had a time when you fasted with others, like Esther, for a community need? What was the outcome? How did it affect your community?

❧

"Nothing can nourish and sustain us like the love of Christ and the power of the Holy Spirit."
—Nicole Unice, *"Esther: Weakness That Leads to Strength,"* Everyday Matters Bible for Women

Points to Ponder

Perhaps the scariest part of coming to God with our deepest needs and desires is the very real possibility he will not grant them. And yet we must come. We need to bring these to him. If we don't, they become idols. They become the thing we bow down to instead of God. Most of the time what we want can be very good, for us and others. There is nothing wrong with these desires. Whether it's something we want for someone else, such as health and safety, and good decisions, or things we desire ourselves—peace, plenty, relief—they still must all be subject to the lordship of Christ.

- What desires or needs have you had that were granted or not granted? How did you respond?

- What are your desires or needs right now? Are you willing to seek God and let him work in your life, no matter what?

Prayer

Before they even exist, my needs are known to you, Lord. Even in the most desperate times, you know the desire of my heart. Prepare me to bring these needs before you, to respond in complete dependence on you.

Add your prayer in your own words.

Amen.

Put It into Practice

Ask God to get your attention and to show you the great needs all around you. Then pray about how you can focus your prayers and fasting toward these needs.

Take-away Treasure

Even when the need is great, the need is not God. As you fast and pray, and seek God's favor in urgent matters, you can rest secure in his control over all things.

For Esther fasting was a sign of humble contrition before God. It was an individual consecration for strength in the face of death and a community cry to God for his intercession. Because of her strength built through fasting, when Esther faced the king, she did so with determination, courage, and grace—and she changed the fate of an entire nation.
    —Nicole Unice, "Esther: Weakness That Leads to Strength," Everyday Matters Bible for Women

Notes / Prayer Requests

_____

_____

_____

_____

_____

_____

_____

_____

_____

_____

_____

_____

_____

_____

_____

_____

_____

Notes / Prayer Requests

Stewardship

CHAPTER 1

The Abundance of the Master

"The Earth Is the Lord's"

They all depend on you
to give them food as they need it.
When you supply it, they gather it.
You open your hand to feed them,
and they are richly satisfied.
But if you turn away from them, they panic.
When you take away their breath,
they die and turn again to dust.
When you give them your breath, life is created,
and you renew the face of the earth.

PSALM 104:27-30

For this study, read Psalm 104.

I grew up in a household characterized by abundance and generosity. I had a room of my own, delicious meals, nice clothing, spending money, and tons of encouragement. Home was a place of peace and plenty. My father especially loved to give good gifts and as much as was in his power to give, he did—which is why it amazes me still what I did the summer I was nine.

I had time on my hands and was rummaging for some reason in my father's side of the bathroom cupboards. Tucked in the back was a jar of change, chock-full of quarters and silver dollars and even some dollar bills. I was astounded at the wealth before me! At which point my darker nature took hold. There were so many coins—surely Dad would not miss a few. The ice cream truck was due any time now and I'd already gone through my allowance. I tucked four quarters into my hand and quietly replaced the jar in the back of the cupboard.

Many, many times that summer I slipped into that jar to supplement my allowance, and from the distance of all these years it's comical to me, but also very sad. I was surrounded by a world of plenty, cloaked in abundance on every level. The riches before my eyes every day far outweighed the coins in that jar, and yet they became what I wanted most— the riches that were not mine. A few years later as a teen, the poverty of my own thinking crystallized in my mind. I was going out with friends, and the cash I needed now far outstripped the resources of the coin jar. I needed $20, so I asked my dad. He pulled $100 out of his wallet, gave it over without a thought, and said, "Have a good time, Sweetie."

God's abundance, and his willingness to shower it upon us, is above and beyond my earthly father's. The natural gifts of air, water, light, and soil—the raw materials of creation and the living beings in our world—all were created by his hand. As Psalm 24:1–2 tells us,

The earth is the LORD's, and everything in it.
The world and all its people belong to him.
For he laid the earth's foundation on the seas
and built it on the ocean depths.

In her article "Stewardship and Entitlement" in the *Everyday Matters Bible for Women*, Holly Vicente Robaina suggests a reason why, in the face of such a generous father, I was silly enough to steal his coins from a jar. She says we face "two great threats today: excessiveness and entitlement."

We have so much we forget who supplied it. And we have so much we feel it must be owed to us—not just owed, but we deserve to have it available when we want it, and only when we want it. Why else would we bother to complain about gifts such as rain, hard work, children, and each other?

There must be another way. Robaina goes on to suggest two disciplines to help us more rightly remember the abundance of God as a gift from God and not what we think we're due: simplicity and stewardship. As she says, "Everything I have is on loan from God, so being careful with his stuff shows him respect." Simplicity asks us to pare down our own needs so we can see the needs of others Stewardship, at its heart of hearts, is a discipline that helps us to rightly remember our position in the family of God. We are not the providers; we are not the suppliers of every good and perfect gift; but neither are we only receivers of those gifts. We also oversee the resources of God for the benefit of his Kingdom.

As we learn the discipline of stewardship, we must start with the abundance of our holdings. God is the author of and the regenerator of all things. All we see, all we hold, has come from him. All we cannot see also comes from him. We will never run out of resources to steward.

"Live simply so others may simply live." —Mother Teresa

> *As you study this chapter, allow yourself time to be grateful. In many ways the study of the abundance of God is our lifelong task as believers.*

1. What did you last complain about? Is there a way to consider the source of the complaint as a gift instead?

2. Take a look at Numbers 18:20, 2 Corinthians 9:6–12, and 1 Chronicles 29:10–17. What do they suggest to you about the abundance of God? What words stand out to you?

3. Among the things we steward is the earth itself. In what ways can you steward the physical world around you?

4. Where in your life can you point to the abundance of God? Think about how greatly he has blessed you.

5. How can you be a blessing to others? What clothes or household items do you no longer use that could benefit someone else?

6. In her novel *Gilead*, Marilynne Robinson writes: "There is more beauty than our eyes can bear; precious things have been put into our hands and to do nothing to honor them is to do great harm." Think about the beauty in your life. What can you do to appreciate it fully and maybe even safeguard it?

"Perhaps it takes a purer faith to praise God for unrealized blessings than for those we once enjoyed or those we enjoy now." —A. W. Tozer

Points to Ponder

In her book *One Thousand Gifts*, Ann Voskamp turned her attention, and the attention of her readers, to the abundance of gifts before us. She began counting them, naming them. But this did not change her life circumstances. People we love still leave us; dreams still disappoint. But she chose to focus on the abundance of the master.

- Where is your focus today?

- List the abundance of gifts you have been given already and give thanks to the Giver.

Prayer

Lord God, Creator of the daily miracles in my life, I thank you. I stand amazed at your love, your never-ending compassion and care for me. May my deeds honor your gifts today.

Add your prayer in your own words.

Amen.

Put It into Practice

Where you are right now, look around. What are the resources you have been given to steward? How many can you name?

Take-away Treasure

One of the best ways to live in and celebrate God's abundance is to get outside, either alone or with a loved one. Feel the weather—sun or rain, cold or heat. Look at the living things sharing the planet with you, and thank God for it all.

We pick a bouquet and we bring it back to the gardener.
—C. S. Lewis

CHAPTER 2

The Role of the Steward

God's Caretakers

When I look at the night sky and see the work of
    your fingers—
    the moon and the stars you set in place—
what are mere mortals that you should think
    about them,
    human beings that you should care for them?
Yet you made them only a little lower than God
    and crowned them with glory and honor.
You gave them charge of everything you made,
    putting all things under their authority—
the flocks and the herds
    and all the wild animals,
the birds in the sky, the fish in the sea,
    and everything that swims the ocean currents.

PSALM 8:3-8

For this study, read Psalm 8.

When it comes to pure escapist enjoyment for me, I love
books and movies with a strong caretaker character.
Whether it's the capable valet Jeeves created by P. G. Wode-
house, or the chauffeur living above the garage in the film

Sabrina, or the housekeeper Alice long ago when I watched *The Brady Bunch*, I love watching these characters go about creating or restoring order to their worlds. They are the other pair of hands and eyes and ears, looking out for the interests of their employers, and as a result providing comfort and assurance in all sorts of ways.

Our Master has given us a caretaker role in this world. So, what is our job description? It's actually pretty straightforward: A steward is one who manages the interests of another, and also acts on behalf of the other. We are managers and agents.

Of course, something is missing from the above definition—the interests of the steward. The only job is to manage the interests of our Master and to make decisions in accordance with his wishes.

As Adele Calhoun states in the *Everyday Matters Bible for Women*, "Stewardship is a vocation—a calling from God in our lives. This calling means that everything I have and am is given to me in trust, to steward for kingdom purposes."

To fulfill our role as stewards, we must first shift our thinking away from what we don't have to what we do have. Even if our finances are scarce, God has given us much to steward.

We have time—sometimes more, sometimes less. We have items we no longer need or use. Sometimes we just have more than we can use. We have our intellect. We can read, write, balance a checkbook, and fill out a form. We have our words and their capacity to bless or curse. We have our redemptive story. We have the earth beneath our feet. We have energy, listening ears, and compassionate embraces. All of these resources of God's are ours to manage on behalf of God, for the benefit of God.

Sometimes what we seem to have, however, is an abundance of pain and loss. Can God mean for us to use that as well? Yes. Even our losses are his to use. As Mary Beth Chapman writes about the death of her young daughter in *Choosing to SEE: A Journey of Struggle and Hope,* "I'm trusting that God saw fit to entrust us to steward this catastrophic loss well. May He be honored with all us Chapmans as we do our best to let the world SEE that He alone is the Author of our salvation, the Mender of our hearts, the Healer of souls."

The paradoxical benefit is that in submitting to the role as steward, we actually benefit ourselves as well. When we see our lives and abilities as the material to be used to further the Kingdom of God, it would be natural to wonder, *But what about me? When do I take care of my own needs?*

We don't. In the process of shaping you as a steward, God also offers the resources for your own needs. He offers true, vital connection with himself and with others. He offers the ultimate stewardship role—that of a family member. When he makes us his children, we are invested in the work of God. When Jesus tells the disciples in Matthew 6:33, "Seek the Kingdom of God above all else, and live righteously, and he will give you everything you need," he is describing the role of the steward—and the rewards.

*"One who cultivates tries to create the
most fertile conditions for good things to
survive and thrive." —Andy Crouch*

**As you study this chapter, it's easy to feel overwhelmed.
We are cultivators of a vast domain, really, and it's easy
to think of all this as just more to do each day. Instead,
let the study and questions reorient your days and your
lists. Find your true work in the world as you study.**

1. Think of your role as steward as focusing on doing the
will of God rather than your own will. What happens to
your own needs as you take pleasing yourself out of the job
description of a steward?

2. When someone agrees to handle something for you, what
do you expect from them? Possibly you expect them to fulfill their promise and to stay in communication with you as
the work progresses. Perhaps we should look at our role as
God's stewards in the same way.

3. Make a list of what you have been given. Be thorough and be detailed. Keep this list where you would keep your daily "to do" list, reminding yourself of the real work of each day.

4. Do you have a painful story God is asking you to steward well? What are the ways you can achieve that?

5. In the *Everyday Matters Bible for Women,* Amy Simpson (quoting from Psalm 50) writes that everything we have is from God. We are indeed caretakers, but God wants us to be "more than just caretakers." How do you see your role as "more than a caretaker"? What does this mean?

6. In the parable of the talents in Matthew 25:14-30, why do you think the master was upset with the servant who hid the money? After all, he did protect it, but as Amy Simpson writes, "that wasn't good enough." What does it mean to really "use these gifts as God would want"?

"Be not simply good; be good for something."
—Henry David Thoreau

Points to Ponder

In her reflection in the *Everyday Matters Bible*, Kara Powell says, "Every dollar we spend is a stewardship decision. . . . We should be mindful of others and try to fund and create systems that offer hope, freedom, and the gospel to people."

- Think about your own daily spending decisions.

- For each decision, think about what it offers to the world. How does it further the desires of God for the earth?

Prayer

Father, I am grateful for the chance to steward your creation, to be a caretaker of all you've put in my charge. I ask you to be my guide and strength in every decision.

Add your prayer in your own words.

Amen.

Put It into Practice

Using the Scriptures as your guide, write yourself a job description as a steward of God. What are your roles and responsibilities? What is your goal?

Take-away Treasure

Becoming a true steward for God isn't just about adding to your responsibilities; it will also mean shedding some projects and plans that don't serve the Master. This week, write down what areas must be shed in order to embrace your role. Once you've written them down, submit them to God, trusting that he will provide a way to have the true desires of your heart, even as you put them aside.

CHAPTER 3

The Confidence of Generosity

"Too Wonderful for Words!"

Honor the LORD with your wealth
  and with the best part of everything you produce.
Then he will fill your barns with grain,
  and your vats will overflow with good wine.

PROVERBS 3:9-10

For this study read 2 Corinthians 9.

At the end of a cross-country flight as I was waiting my turn to disembark, a man and his son began shuffling toward me. As they allowed others to file out before them, the father tousled his son's hair and gave him a paraphrase of Matthew 20:16: "Don't worry—in the end, the first shall be last and the last shall be first." The boy looked ahead at the people filing off the plane and said to us all, "Well, today, the first are first and the last are just last!"

Our role as stewards of God's Kingdom will often put us last. People will push in front of us, literally and figuratively, to gain an advantage of time, money, or attention. And it's easy to believe what the *Adversary* would like us to believe: We live in a world of scarcity. From jobs to affection to limited-time offers, if it's going to happen it's going to be up to us and our ingenuity to get it done. We are constantly reminded that there is only so much of anything to go around.

Trusting God alone is part and parcel of all the work of the disciplines. Each discipline calls us back to this essential truth of living life with God, empowered by God and not us. Trusting God enough to be generous to others takes both our attention and our submission. It also takes our imagination. We have to envision the world as *God* sees it: As a place of abundance. We have to reject the images of scarcity so prevalent in our culture. Not only is there enough—there is more than enough. And perhaps that's why in 1 Timothy 6:17–19, Paul gives us something to put in our minds to replace the world's vision of scarcity:

> *Teach those who are rich in this world not to be proud and not to trust in their money, which is so unreliable. Their trust should be in God, who richly gives us all we need for our enjoyment. Tell them to use their money to do good. They should be rich in good works and generous to those in need, always being ready to share with others. By doing this they will be storing up their treasure as a good foundation for the future so that they may experience true life.*

We need this image—of being rich in good works, of storing up a different kind of treasure. Our Lord knows we don't work well when we have emptied ourselves of a bad way of thinking but don't have something positive to put in its place.

As much as the role of steward is about the resources we have been given by God, there are two things with which we should not confuse it. Stewardship is not about tithing, about giving back to God the firstfruits of our work. That is certainly another discipline, one we take seriously as disciples of Christ. Tithing is part of our stewardship, but it is not the totality of it. Stewardship involves *all* of our resources, not just a portion. And though stewardship is about how we use what we have, it's also trusting God for our future needs. Stewardship may be done wisely and with deliberation, but it isn't hoarding. All of Scripture is consistent about the generosity of God, about pouring out our lives for others. As Hebrews 13:5–6 tells us,

> *Don't love money; be satisfied with what you have. For God has said,*
>
> > *"I will never fail you.*
> > *I will never abandon you."*
>
> *So we can say with confidence,*
>
> > *"The Lord is my helper,*
> > *so I will have no fear.*
> > *What can mere people do to me?"*

How do we navigate being generous and yet wise with the gifts of God? When does our generosity become foolishness? I believe this is where paying attention is the key. We must examine our motives. What is compelling our actions?

If we are generous, is it to be noticed? Jesus' words and judgment are strong and swift in this regard:

> *"Watch out! Don't do your good deeds publicly, to be admired by others, for you will lose the reward from your Father in heaven. When you give to someone in need, don't do as the hypocrites do—blowing trumpets in the synagogues and streets to call attention to their acts of charity! I tell you the truth, they have received all the reward they will ever get. But when you give to someone in need, don't let your left hand know what your right hand is doing. Give your gifts in private, and your Father, who sees everything, will reward you."* *(Matthew 6:1–4)*

Conversely, our hesitancy to be generous should also be examined. Is it because there are better opportunities? Or is it a fear of scarcity, of not having enough? In the end, it is the motive and not the action alone that interests God. Remember, he is the source of everything. He is not in need of our generosity. But he knows how essential it is for us to give *all* of our lives—our time, our talents, and our futures—over to him.

―――――――――― ❧ ――――――――――

"Like the tree who grows where he's planted, we need not launch a search party to discover who we are. Stay right where you are, as you are, complete in your identity as an image bearer and reach up your arms to God, reflecting his glory with your life." —Emily P. Freeman

As you study this chapter, think of how far God has shepherded you on your faith journey— the ways he cares for your needs, both large and small. Remember, he can be trusted.

1. In his book *Counterfeit Gods,* Timothy Keller talks about deep idols, powerful concepts that fuel more superficial idols such as money or relationships. He writes, "Each deep idol—power, approval, comfort or control—generates a different set of fears and a different set of hopes." Think about times you have been fearful of acting generously. Are there deeper idols at stake for you? What might they be?

2. In 2 Corinthians 8:2–4, Paul reports on the generosity of the Macedonian churches, even in their poverty. Think about times you've hesitated to be generous and the reasons why. In light of the biblical examples of generosity, do your reasons make sense?

3. Romans 5:1–11 is a litany of the generous gifts of God. Read through this passage and think of all the gifts given to you through faith.

4. Think about times when you were generous in spite of your circumstances. What was the outcome? Did you find God's provision surpassed what you yourself could have done?

5. In "Stewardship of Time" in the *Everyday Matters Bible for Women*, Patricia Mitchell talks about the importance of time, and of balancing our lives between trying to do too much and what God really wants us to do. How are you spending your time? Are there better ways you could be using it?

6. Think about the time (minutes, hours, days) you have quietly given toward the work of the Kingdom—whether through church ministry or praying with a friend in need. Did you find it rewarding? Has this encouraged you to spend your time more generously?

"God is not glorified when we keep for ourselves (no matter how thankfully) what we ought to be using to alleviate the misery of unevangelized, uneducated, unmedicated, and unfed millions." —John Piper

Points to Ponder

Sometimes generosity as a steward is hard because we want the recipients to be worthy. We want them to deserve this great gift we're passing along from the living God. And when they don't respond with the gratitude we think is due, we get resentful. Or perhaps, because of past conflict, we struggle to forgive someone for their part in creating the need in the first place.

- Although we're confident in God, we're less confident in ourselves and the people we're serving. How do we move past such feelings?

- One way of moving past such feelings is to bring them to the cross. Can you admit your own need for grace and the good news of salvation? Can you trust the outcome to God?

Prayer

Lord, I depend on you for all my needs. When I am tempted to hoard and take control, stop me. It is not what I truly want, and it does not reflect who I truly am. Direct me in the good work you have given me.

Add your prayer in your own words.

Amen.

Put It into Practice

Often our actions speak louder than words, telling ourselves and others what we really think about God. Can he really be trusted to provide for us? Can we really rest in his care? Take a look at your calendar and your checkbook. Do they speak of a steward generously acting on behalf of the Master? If not, you may want to rethink and pray about positive change.

Take-away Treasure

Giving generously, with the full confidence in the abundance of God, can be a joy. But it doesn't have to be haphazard. If you're a planner, go ahead and plan. As a steward, find a need you feel called to address. Map out a plan to help with the resources you have. Enjoy your role as a steward!

> *As a result of your ministry, they will give glory to God. For your generosity to them and to all believers will prove that you are obedient to the Good News of Christ. And they will pray for you with deep affection because of the overflowing grace God has given to you. Thank God for this gift too wonderful for words! (2 Corinthians 9:13–15)*

CHAPTER 4

Growth Is the Goal

Not Playing It "Safe"

"To those who use well what they are given,
even more will be given, and they will have an
abundance. But from those who do nothing,
even what little they have will be taken away."

MATTHEW 25:29

For this study, read Matthew 25:14–46.

The seminal passage in the Bible, one worth returning to
again and again as we learn the discipline of stewardship,
is the parable of the talents told in Matthew 25:14–28 and
Luke 19:12–27. Three servants are each given an amount
to invest on their master's behalf. And it's a significant
amount—the equivalent of over two million dollars today.
Two of the servants do as the master asks and double the
amount they were given. One does nothing. He risks nothing, loses nothing—but gains nothing either.

In Michael Card's *Matthew: The Gospel of Identity*, he says
this parable has to do with "confusion regarding the true
character of the master." Jesus is about to leave and his

return will be in a long while. Those who serve him well cannot conceive, truly, of the joy they will encounter when upon his return he says, "Well done, my good and faithful servant. You have been faithful in handling this small amount, so now I will give you many more responsibilities. Let's celebrate together!" (Matthew 25:21). At the same time, Card writes, "Some will be afraid at his coming because they never really understood his loving-kindness. Though they might try to use their confusion as an excuse for their lack of fruit, they will not be excused."

The reward for growing the Kingdom, according to the parable, is more responsibility and a joyous celebration with the Master. The punishment for not growing the Kingdom is abandonment by the Master. What we have is taken and, even more importantly, the presence of the Master is taken from us. This is a parable meant to stop us in our tracks and consider the goal of the Master: growth. That is the only result rewarded.

As the time of Jesus' earthly ministry drew to its close, he used his teachings again and again to talk about what was expected of the disciples in his absence. He expected them to be careful stewards, watching for his return but faithfully caring for others in his charge (Matthew 24:45).

Jesus spoke to a people who had been raised in a world hemmed in by layers of law, all aimed at making sure nothing changed. Some were interested in the restoration of a Kingdom, but just as many were interested in maintaining the status quo. And while the original motive of the Pharisees—hundreds of years before the birth of Christ—was a stubborn refusal to abandon God and embrace the Greek beliefs, by the time of Christ the rigid set of rules and regulations no longer reflected their true identity. They had *become* their identity. In addition, as Eugene Peterson states in *The Jesus Way*, "The Pharisees had become small-minded, obsessively concerned with all the minute details of personal behavior."

Think about conversations you have with other believers. Think about the decisions made in your small group, in your committees—any place where you decide, as stewards, what will be done or not done as the body of Christ. In the context of the parable of the talents, we should all be wary of any decision aimed at keeping things just the same. Growth is the only goal of the Kingdom of God.

In Jesus' parable, what's also striking is that growth is the only outcome of the investments of the first two servants. From our perspective, we think of investing as an activity laden with risk. We might gain, we might lose. With the prompting of our Adversary, we are very used to considering the path of failure. We can usually provide a vivid picture of what it looks like to risk and fail. But for God, using his talents to further his Kingdom yields only one result: growth. Take heart in this good news—every decision aimed at growing God's Kingdom produces fruit. While it might not take the form we envision, it is there nonetheless. The only way we can fail is if we refuse to grow.

As you study this chapter, plan on reading through both versions of this parable several times (Matthew 25:14–28 and Luke 19:12–27). Meditate on the words, pray, and allow this story to become your story.

1. What ways do you find yourself acting like the third servant, fearful of change or risk in your faith life? Why?

2. Consider the assets you are stewarding at present. Choose just one of them and consider what it would mean to invest it for growth of God's Kingdom.

3. The third servant in the parable considers the master to be a hard man. Do you find yourself considering God in the same way? The servant is also afraid of risk because he's afraid to lose. What are you afraid of losing?

4. Why do you think the master in the parable gives different amounts to the servants?

5. In "The Calling of True Stewardship" in the *Everyday Matters Bible for Women*, Adele Ahlberg Calhoun writes: "Being a steward has not come naturally to me. The phrase *we can't afford that* has shaped my heart into what a counselor called 'deprivation neurosis.' I fear not having enough for later. Not to put too fine a point upon it, but stewarding my resources can make me nervous. . . . But I don't want to trust God *less* the more I have." Is there any "deprivation neurosis" in your life? If so, how can you overcome it?

6. Think about the ways in which you have hid yourself away—like the third servant did with the talents given to him. How can you be more like the other two servants?

"As stewards, we have no right to squander, hoard, treasure, ignore, abuse, or merely protect what God has entrusted to us. We're obligated to use these gifts as God would want. God gives us gifts not merely for our pleasure, but for his pleasure and glory." —Amy Simpson

Points to Ponder

Sometimes we find it easier to be faithful when we have little than when we have a lot of anything. But what if God chose you, as in the parable of the servants, to be given a larger portion of God's Kingdom to steward?

- How can you stay true to the desire for the kind of Kingdom growth God requires and not begin to seek instead to maintain your own position allowed by your resources, whether they are finances, influence, or skills?

- What practices will keep you serving God from a place of plenty as well as a place of need?

Prayer

Father, I want to be a steward in word and deed. I want to grow your Kingdom and celebrate its growth when Jesus returns. Grant me wisdom to invest my talents and trust you to achieve the results you desire.

Add your prayer in your own words.

Amen.

Put It into Practice

Today, place a coin before you. Let it represent for you the many gifts you've been given by God to steward well. Every time you see it, ask yourself: What can I do *today* to grow the Kingdom?

Take-away Treasure

Envision yourself as each of the stewards in Jesus' parable. What would it look like for you to be the first steward? The second? The third? Write down in as much detail as possible what they might feel, what helped them make their decisions, how you would invest (or not) and why.

> *Offering myself and my resources to God daily is the calling of true stewardship. Stewards risk that they can't out-give God. . . . There are always people who need something we steward for God: time, money, gifts, talents, cars, airline miles, hotel credits, houses, and on. Will we share? Will we invite God to use these resources for his purposes, not ours?* —Adele Ahlberg Calhoun, "The Calling of True Stewardship," Everyday Matters Bible for Women

Notes / Prayer Requests

Notes / Prayer Requests

Leader's Guide

to Fasting & Stewardship

Thoughts on Where to Meet

* If you have the chance, encourage each group member to host a gathering. But make sure your host knows that you don't expect fresh baked scones from scratch or white-glove-test-worthy surroundings. Set the tone for a relaxed and open atmosphere with a warm welcome wherever you can meet. The host can provide the space and the guests can provide the goodies.

* If you can't meet in homes, consider taking at least one of your meetings on the road. Can you meet at a local place where people from your community gather? A park or a coffee shop or other public space perhaps.

* If you meet in a church space, consider partnering with another local church group and take turns hosting. How can you extend your welcome outside your group?

Thoughts on Ways to Foster Welcome

- If many of your members have a hard time meeting
  due to circumstances, look for ways to work around
  it. Consider providing childcare if there are moms
  who have difficulty attending, or meet in an acces-
  sible space if someone who might want to join has a
  disability. Does a morning time work better? Could
  you meet as smaller groups and then get together as
  a larger group for an event? Be flexible and see how
  you can accommodate the needs of the group. Incorporate "get to know you" activities to promote sharing. Don't take yourselves too seriously and let your
  humor shine through.

Incorporating Other Practices

- *Lift your voices.* Integrate worship throughout
  the study. Find songs that speak of fasting and
  stewardship.

- *Commit to lift each other up in prayer.* You may want
  to have a prayer walk as part of seeing opportunities
  to serve in your community, or prayer partners who
  might be able to meet at other times.

- *Dig deep into the word.* Take the study at your own
  pace but consider including passages for participants
  to read in between meetings. The *Everyday Matters
  Bible for Women* has a wealth of additional resources.

- *Celebrate!* Bring cupcakes and candles, balloons or anything celebratory to distribute to each member of the group. Ask each person to share something that they want to celebrate today, be it an event, a new insight, or anything they choose.

Fasting & Stewardship

The disciplines of fasting and stewardship can be fraught with tension for a believer, and leading a group to discuss them can pose many challenges. Be encouraged—the benefits of the disciplines are well worth it for your group, but you will need to navigate patiently and direct the study with care. Here are a few suggestions as you lead:

- Resist the temptation to spend time on "how to." Because both these disciplines can easily become a "checklist faith," plan your time together to be rich in the reading of Scripture and the focus on motivation. Keep any detail-oriented questions open-ended, with the possibility of many "right" answers.

- Encourage storytelling but don't allow excuses. This is not a time for the group to give reasons why they can't undertake the discipline. It's a time to explore together what it means to practice the discipline, and to do that we need to tell our stories. Ask your group to talk about the emotions that come to mind when they think of fasting or stewardship. Ask for stories behind the emotions. Bring those stories to Scripture and each other so that group members can test for themselves the validity of their emotions.

- Pray before you meet, and as a group, for a discussion free of judgment. We easily fall into the comparison trap when it comes to how we spend our time and money, and how "godly" our experiences are. We must remember that our Adversary would like nothing better than to pull us apart, for us to stop meeting together to encourage one another. Your goal is growth of disciples. Create, with God's help, an atmosphere of no judgment, but also one that challenges each member to pursue righteousness with her whole heart.

- Bring in visual tools to provide an added anchor to your discussions. Maybe as you talk about fasting, you can bring in a typical day's food supply for a first-century believer. Or as you discuss stewardship, bring in things that cost about two dollars each, which represents a full day's wages for most of the world. Or place crayons, model clay, or other art supplies in the room. As you discuss the abundance of God and the things you steward, group members can draw or create representations of those items to take home.

- Listen to the needs of the group. It could be that your group is discussing fasting at a time when one member has a critical need. Be open to the working of the Spirit to use your group to seek God's favor, or to grow God's Kingdom together.

- Add other spiritual disciplines to your discussions. As you study fasting, consider also the disciplines of Bible study and meditation, confession, contemplation, forgiveness, prayer, submission, and worship. For your time together on the discipline of stewardship, you might want to bring in further disciplines of simplicity, service, Sabbath and rest, justice, gratitude, and community.

Follow Up

Each of us is on a journey of discipleship. We will all attempt things that fail, or stumble our way through our service to God. As your group finishes your time together, make sure to stay in touch and encourage one another.

Additional Resources

* *Christians in an Age of Wealth: A Biblical Theology of Stewardship* by Craig L. Blomberg

* *The Daniel Fast* by Susan Gregory (www.danielfast. wordpress.com)

* See www.Economicdiscipleship.com

* *Every Good Endeavor: Connecting Your Work to God's Work* by Timothy Keller

* *Fasting for Spiritual Breakthrough: A Guide to Nine Biblical Fasts* by Elmer Towns

* *A Hunger for God: Desiring God Through Fasting and Prayer* by John Piper

- *The Jesus Way: A Conversation on the Ways That Jesus Is the Way* by Eugene H. Peterson

- *Matthew: The Gospel of Identity* by Michael Card

- *Money, Possessions and Eternity* by Randy Alcorn

EVERYDAY MATTERS BIBLE STUDIES
for women

Spiritual practices for everyday life

Acceptance	Mentoring
Bible Study & Meditation	Outreach
Celebration	Prayer
Community	Reconciliation
Confession	Sabbath & Rest
Contemplation	Service
Faith	Silence
Fasting	Simplicity
Forgiveness	Solitude
Gratitude	Stewardship
Hospitality	Submission
Justice	Worship

HENDRICKSON
PUBLISHERS

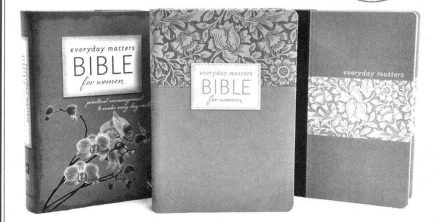